Blue Peacock—*Papilio polymnestor*

...nor

...ker Swallowtail—
Papilio dardanus

Paper Kite—
Idea leuconoe

Pansy—
Precis westermani

Lacewing—*Cethosia hypsea*

Mountain Blue Swallowtail—
Papilio ulysses

Purple Tips—*Colotis ione*

Paradise Birdwing—
Ornithoptera paradisea

Peacock Pansy—*Precis almana*

Citrus Swallowtail—*Papilio demoleus*

Tailed Jay—
Graphium agamemnon

Fabulous Fluttering TROPICAL BUTTERFLIES

Dorothy Hinshaw Patent

ILLUSTRATIONS BY Kendahl Jan Jubb

WALKER & COMPANY
NEW YORK

To the child in each of us, who always loves butterflies. —D.P.

For Hattie & Satchel, my two newest butterflies. —K.J.

First published in the United States of America in 2003 by Walker Publishing Company, Inc.

Published simultaneously in Canada by Fitzhenry and Whiteside, Markham, Ontario L3R 4T8

For information about permission to reproduce selections from this book, write to Permissions, Walker & Company, 435 Hudson Street, New York, New York 10014

Library of Congress Cataloging-in-Publication Data
Patent, Dorothy Hinshaw.
    Fabulous fluttering tropical butterflies / Dorothy Hinshaw Patent; illustrations by Kendahl Jan Jubb.
    p. cm.
    Summary: Describes the physical characteristics and behavior of various kinds of tropical butterflies.
    ISBN 0-8027-8838-6 (hc)—ISBN 0-8027-8839-4 (re)
    1. Butterflies—Tropics—Juvenile literature. 2. Rain forest animals—Juvenile literature. [1. Butterflies.
    2. Rain forest animals.] I. Jubb, Kendahl Jan, ill. II. Title.
QL560.6 .P38 2002
595.78'9'0913—dc21

                                                    2002024982

The illustrations for this book were done in Windsor Newton watercolors on Arches 140-lb. paper.

Book design by Maura Fadden Rosenthal /Mspace

Visit Walker & Company's Web site at www.walkerbooks.com

Printed in Hong Kong

10 9 8 7 6 5 4 3 2 1

Glittering butterflies flit across meadows and through forests around the world. Bright green, flaming red, flashing blue—every color of the rainbow decorates their graceful wings.

Butterflies love warmth, and the plants that feed them thrive on moisture. So tropical rain forests make especially good homes for butterflies, including the largest and flashiest butterflies in the world.

Even the biggest butterfly
starts out as a speck-sized egg,
which will hatch into a tiny caterpillar.
The female butterfly lays her eggs carefully
on or nearby the kind of plant her caterpillars will
eat. The caterpillar is an eating machine, munching its
way through leaves and growing, growing, growing. As it
gets bigger, its skin gets too tight. It sheds the old
skin and gets a new one that is large enough for its
body, and then some.

Eat, grow, shed. Eat, grow, shed—that's
the life of the caterpillar. In just two
weeks, it can grow to 30,000 times
its original size!

In some species, the
new skin is a different color from
the old one. Some caterpillars develop
stripes that hide them on leaves. Others
grow protective spines and fuzzy prickles.

When it has finished growing, the caterpillar finds a hidden spot. There it spins a silk button to anchor itself, then sheds its skin one last time. Now it has become a chrysalis, which looks completely different from the caterpillar or the butterfly. The chrysalis of most butterflies is brown or green, but some are gleaming gold.

The chrysalis hangs quietly and looks lifeless. But inside its protective covering, the crawling, munching caterpillar with sixteen legs is changing into a flying, drinking butterfly with just six legs.

Usually in about two weeks, the hard shell of the
chrysalis thins, revealing the colorful butterfly inside.
Within a few days, the chrysalis splits. The butterfly crawls
out, its wings crumpled and folded alongside its body.

8

The perfect new butterfly hangs
on a stem, pumping blood
from its body into the veins
on its wings. Bit by bit, the wings
spread open and harden.

Once its wings have hardened, the
butterfly flies off, ready to explore its
surroundings.

The colors and
designs of its wings are made by
countless tiny scales arranged like
roofing tiles, 250 to the inch. Black, brown,
red, white, and yellow come from colored
material called pigment, which is located in the
scales. Blue, green, gold, and silver aren't made
from pigment. Instead, they are tricks of light,
formed as the light glances off microscopic
ridges on the scales.

Morphos are the largest butterflies in Central and South America. They can have a wingspan of more than nine inches. Some male morphos are among the most brilliantly colored butterflies in the world. The bright blue of their upper wings flashes in the sunlight as they flit through the forest, attracting females along the way. But when they land, they seem to disappear. How does that happen?

When he lands,
the morpho closes his wings,
showing their brown-patterned
undersides. They become camouflaged,
blending in perfectly with the light and
shadow of the forest floor. Close-up,
however, the pattern has spots that look like
eyes. A bird that finds the butterfly might be
attracted to the bright eyespot and peck there on
the wing instead of aiming its bite at the soft body.
A butterfly with tattered wings can survive just fine,
but one with a wounded body will become a
bird's meal.

The bright colors of some caterpillars and butterflies are a warning—"Don't eat me!" These butterflies gather poisons from the plants they eat while they are caterpillars. The poisons don't hurt either the caterpillars or the butterflies, but they can make birds sick. One nip at the wing of a poisonous butterfly and the bird remembers not to eat another one like it again.

13

Tropical butterflies known as longwings warn of their bad taste with red or yellow spots and blotches on their wings. The postman butterfly is an example of a longwing.

Butterflies that taste just fine have come to imitate poisonous kinds like the postman. Birds can't tell the difference, so they also leave the "copycats" alone.

Many kinds of butterflies copy the postman. Several different species, some poisonous and some tasty, may all look alike. A cluster of butterflies gathered on a moist spot on the forest floor might look identical but might actually contain four or more different species.

Although most
butterflies live only a
few weeks, some longwings
can survive for as long as nine
months. Most butterflies drink
only sugary nectar from flowers or
feed on rotting fruit. But these
longwings also eat pollen.
The pollen gives
them protein,
which helps
them live so long.

Longwings also have especially good eyesight. The females use their sharp eyes to spot caterpillars or the eggs of other females on their food plants, almost always a kind of passion flower vine. If the female sees caterpillars or eggs on a particular vine, she won't lay her own eggs there. Her youngsters will need plenty to eat, so they don't need any competition for the available food. Besides, these fierce caterpillars may eat one another!

17

Tropical swallowtails come in all sorts of colors. They can be deep yellow, brilliant red, bright blue, or gleaming green, usually combined with velvety black.

The African mocker swallowtail got its name by mocking, or copying, several other kinds of butterflies. Male mockers look like typical swallowtails, with black-and-creamy-white wings. In some places, the females look much like the males. Elsewhere, however, the females come in different colors and even different sizes. More than 100 different versions of tailless female mockers live in different parts of Africa and copy different distasteful butterflies. They can be black and orange, orange and white, or almost completely black.

The giant birdwings are related to swallowtails. These brilliantly colored fliers live on isolated Pacific Islands, such as New Guinea. Male birdwings are decorated in brilliant blue, green, yellow, or orange and black. Some have graceful slender tails on their hind wings. The larger females are mostly brown and white.

The rare Queen Alexandra birdwing is the largest butterfly in the world. The female's brown-and-white wings can span more than eleven inches. The wings of the smaller males gleam in bright green, rich blue, and deep black on top and green and gold underneath.

Like the longwings, the Queen Alexandra birdwing feeds on pollen as well as nectar. These powerful insects fly high above the ground, cruising the top of the forest canopy looking for flowers.

Some owl butterflies, which live in Central and South America, are almost as big as morphos and birdwings. Their name comes from the especially big eyespots on the undersides of the hind wings. If you look upside down at an owl butterfly with its wings spread out, it looks like the face of an owl. Markings on the wings around the "eyes" even resemble feathers.

Thousands of other kinds of beautiful butterflies also live in the tropics, and they have names like crackers, crows, jays, pansies, and queens.

You don't have to travel to faraway lands to see these tropical gems. All over North America, parks and zoos are building big greenhouses where people can experience the world of the tropical butterfly.

Tropical butterflies need special conditions in order to survive away from their natural environment. The temperature inside these butterfly houses must be kept warm. The air needs to be damp, just as it is in a tropical rain forest. The greenhouse walls help collect heat from the sun during the day, and heaters help warm the building at night. Nozzles spray a fine mist to add moisture to the air, and fans keep the air moving so that the warmth and moistness spread evenly. Ponds and small waterfalls can add both beauty and moisture to a butterfly house.

Beautiful plants in the house
give the butterflies places to land, and their flowers
provide nectar. Winding paths allow human visitors to
wander slowly, exploring the miniature forest and
looking for winged
treasures.

If you visit a butterfly house, it's important to be quiet and to stay on the paths. Try standing still for a moment—maybe a black-and-white paper kite will land on your shoulder or even on your hand, especially if you're wearing flower colors like yellow, blue, or red.

Bend down and look
among the leaves.
A big owl butterfly may
be resting there. Sit on a
bench and watch the butterflies
flutter and zoom. Look for a tray of
old bananas or cut apples. See which
butterflies feed on them.

Most butterfly houses have a
display of chrysalises waiting to
split open so the butterflies can
emerge. If you are lucky, you might
see a brilliant lacewing struggle out
of its chrysalis and spread its wings.

Since most tropical butterflies live for only two to eight weeks, how does a butterfly house in Ohio or New York keep getting these delicate tropical gems? Butterfly farms in tropical countries raise the caterpillars, then send the chrysalises far and wide for people around the world to enjoy. At the same time, butterfly farms protect tropical forests and meadows by providing homes for wild butterflies.

The Butterfly Farm in Costa Rica sends out 50,000 chrysalises each year. Workers there have planted thousands of plants that provide food for caterpillars and nectar for butterflies. They catch a few of the butterflies and put them inside netted areas. Protected inside the netting, the insects feed, mate, and lay their eggs. The workers collect the tiny eggs. When the eggs hatch, the little caterpillars are fed on the kind of leaves they normally eat.

After these caterpillars become
chrysalises, they are shipped to
butterfly houses throughout the world,
where they hatch out into colorful flying jewels
that we can all enjoy.

Index of Butterflies in this Book
(with scientific names)

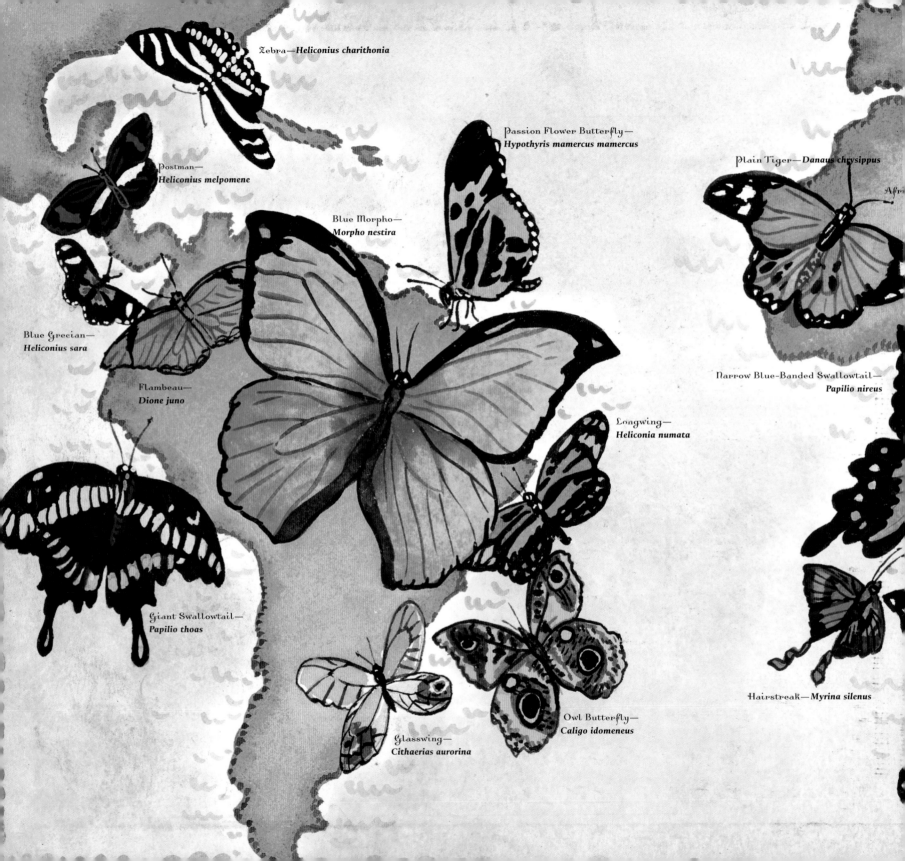

Zebra—*Heliconius charithonia*

Postman—
Heliconius melpomene

Passion Flower Butterfly—
Hypothyris mamercus mamercus

Plain Tiger—*Danaus chrysippus*

Afr

Blue Morpho—
Morpho nestira

Blue Grecian—
Heliconius sara

Narrow Blue-Banded Swallowtail—
Papilio nireus

Flambeau—
Dione juno

Longwing—
Heliconia numata

Giant Swallowtail—
Papilio thoas

Glasswing—
Cithaerias aurorina

Owl Butterfly—
Caligo idomeneus

Hairstreak—*Myrina silenus*